Winter

Prague Winter

Gerda Mayer

Hearing Eye

Published by Hearing Eye 2005

Hearing Eye
Box 1, 99 Torriano Avenue
London NW5 2RX, UK
email: hearing_eye@torriano.org
www.torriano.org

ISBN: 1870841 12 3

Acknowledgements
Extracts from *Prague Winter* appeared in *Writers' Awards 2001*,
The Arts Council of England, and in *New Writing 10*,
Picador/The British Council.

Unseen was first published in *Manifold* 1969; *Children with Candles*, in
Ambit, 1990; *Seafarer* from 'Time Watching' (Hearing Eye, 1995) first
published in *Ambit*, 1983; *Fragment* first published in *Ariel*, 1971;
Anon in *The Spectator*, 1987; *All the Leaves* in *The Knockabout Show*,
Chatto Poets for the Young, Chatto & Windus, 1978;
Dinosaur Footprints Unearthed In Swanage in *Ambit*, 1988.

This publication has been made possible with
the financial support of Arts Council England

Printed by Aldgate Press, London

Designed by Martin Parker at silbercow.co.uk

To the friends of my childhood

(Some of the names have been changed)

Unseen

Present met Past,
Said: I am your Future.
But Past walked by
Without look or gesture.

Present then strained
To define Past's nature,
But his sight was too short
To catch every feature.

While Present looked back
Absorbed in the creature,
Future walked by;
Unseen; without gesture.

The Brown House

The house where I was born. House Kerag in Karlsbad. Later, the Nazi headquarters, so my mother informed me. And one night, it is September 1938, a great wave of sound erupts from that house, deep, hoarse chants of *Siegheil* that spill over, that flood the entire town, that reach out to us on the outskirts, as if the house of my birth had turned against me: a chant threatening and terrible from which I must flee. The name of some colour it had now. *Das braune Haus*, was it? The Brown House?

The Czech authorities have imposed martial law and my parents are not yet at home. The chant of *Siegheil*, ecstatic and fanatic, continues as if it will never end. Marie, our cook, wants to be off, to spend the alarming night with a friend. Although a 'big' girl of eleven, I beg her not to leave me alone in the flat. So she agrees to deposit me first at my grandmother's. The September night is bright and starlit – though perhaps I am remembering quite another night altogether.

Arrived at my grandmother's, I find – oh the relief – my parents with her, in quiet, sombre conversation. I am prepared for jollifications at this happy reunion, but their mood does not lift. My parents return home with me.

A Rude Man

People are consulting each other about the imminent invasion of the Sudeten. My father tries to consult another small Jewish shopkeeper in the street of shops. 'How do I know! How am I to know what to do! Why does everyone come to me for advice?' roars that reluctant guru at my father. (Who knows? perhaps his shop is a smidgin larger, more prosperous, than the other little shops in the street; perhaps in normal times he was a man to be looked up to…). Now he fairly dances with self-importance, with assumed exasperation, in the middle of the street. He puffs himself up. – But then, indeed, how is he to know?

Farewell

'Home' is where we moved to when I was a year-and-a-half: a rented flat in a fairly graceless house, clad in rust-coloured roughcast, that calls itself a 'villa'. No ancestral home has ever been more beloved, but at this moment, as 'little girl walks through the rooms, bidding farewell to the home of her childhood', is there not a tiny voice somewhere that cries 'hurray!'?

'The Czechs will throw Hitler out in a week,' my mother predicts. Even so – a week's holiday from school! And, who knows, Hitler might oblige and stay a full fortnight. Perhas, too, in subterranean consciousness, the lights of Prague beckon, romantic poverty and adventure.

So we are on the train to Prague, shortly before Hitler annexes the Sudeten, the German-speaking part of Czechoslovakia. I allow another child to play with my doll; a less generous act than it might appear, as this doll is my least favoured.

At my Aunt's

In Prague we separate. My parents go to to one aunt, I and Waldi, our dachshund, to another. I am allowed to sleep in a drawer on the floor – a thrill and a treat. This is adventure indeed.

My uncle-by-marriage tends to bellow at me; my Aunt Mizzi, in her indolent, good-natured fashion, and with barely a word said, indicates that I am a pain. My handsome, red-headed, gangly cousin Heinz has already entered the land of grown-ups and girls. 'So each table has a telephone and, when a man wants to ask a girl for a dance, he just rings her up at her table and requests the pleasure.' It falls to my cousin Anneliese who is 'good with children' to take me in hand.

Anneliese, sixteen, is pretty and jolly, with bouncy curls and big brown eyes. She is a poet and a teller of stories that sometimes entertain and sometimes horrify. She is a great favourite and much more fun than my own elder sister. Nevertheless...

The Refugee Dog

We are at the butcher's, Anneliese and I, to buy Waldi, our dachshund, a sausage. It is his one meal of the day. Anneliese glances – first at the butcher and then – meaningfully – at the dog. As usual, Waldi patiently carries the sausage home in his mouth. And suddenly I notice things moving in the sausage, white, terrible, filthy things, and realize that the sausage is full of maggots. 'Look, – oh look!' (Oh my poor dear dog.) But my cousin feigns deaf and walks on.

Eventually, my parents, my elder sister and I move to a couple of rented rooms. Waldi stays behind.

(And later, in England, when I pray for my family before falling asleep, I shall be including Waldi in my prayers; and I shall ask about him in my letters back home. Then, one day, my mother, perhaps to reassure me, will draw a picture of our dog in one of her letters. He is a dachshund but she has given him pointed ears. She has not only not seen him for a long time, she has forgotten what he looked like, she has even forgotten what breed of dog he was... And I, in my letters home, shall not be mentioning my dog again.)

Digs

There are beetles in the lavatory that go plop when I cruelly crush them underfoot; PLOP like those white berries on a certain bush in the garden back home, those little white explosives.

My father has mistaken our digs for a hotel. 'I warned you not to put your shoes out at night!' my mother mildly remonstrates, after a scolding from our landlady. The rooms are dingy, without cooking facilities or running water. At one stage, my father and I have to share a narrow bed, lying sardine fashion, my father complaining at the way I thrash about.

My father turns out to be somewhat more

domesticated than my mother. Cream cheese on apple is a delicacy, he instructs me.

When I do the washing-up, crouching over a basin on the floor, he is quite put out when I immerse the silver handles of the knives in water. 'They'll come off.'

My mother rises above such mundane matters. She stands thoughtfully in the middle of the room, gently swishing a broom to and fro, as if uncertain what to do with so esoteric a device. Among other efforts at emigration, she is thinking of going to England on a domestic permit. Moreover, she is learning to make leather flowers, a possibly useful skill in a foreign country.

And then, suddenly, she is offered a proper job, but here in Prague, as a designer of knitwear. She would have to promise to stay with the firm for two years. So she is obliged to turn the job down.

A Dip into the Past

My sister, my half-sister, is blonde, blue-eyed, and extremely pretty. She is my mother's daughter by her first marriage to handsome Hans.

'I'm going to my wedding now, Papa.' But grandfather went on shaving. 'I'm going to my wedding now, Papa.' Nevertheless, my mother

'Anne'

married her handsome but feckless Hans. And her parents came round in the end and mother got her substantial dowry after all. Handsome Hans blew the lot, in two months flat, whoopee!

Two years later, my mother divorced him, firmly but without rancour on her side. Indeed, she is said to have walked in the forest, writing poems to his memory, it being often easier to esteem someone retrospectively than in the troublesome present. She returned with my beautiful sister to her parental home, until she met and married my father.

But as for Anne, she wears a little gold cross at her throat, and feels a very changeling. How unfair that her lot has been cast among the Jews.

And, no, Mother, she can't take Gerti along: Gerti isn't wearing gloves. She does not say, 'I can't take Gerti along, she'd be a dead give-away.' So it's Gerti (aged nine or ten at the time) isn't wearing gloves. Mother goes along with the euphemism.

Ablutions

Our digs in Prague do not run to a bathroom. My sister, Anne, is standing naked at the wash-stand, with her back to my mother and me. Her small waist curves gently outward at the hips. My mother who feels that I never do my elder sister justice exhorts me to admire her.

'Oh Mother, really...' says Anne.

On another occasion, with the family assembled, I dance around in the nude.

'Mother, how can you allow Gerti to caper around like this in front of father?' And, in the silence that ensues, there is a sort of embarrassment. For already I am sprouting breasts.

Very soon Prague loses its glamour and I am homesick.

'I wish I were back in Karlsbad,' I confide to my diary. 'If only Hitler weren't there. He's very disagreeable.'

Background

The German Jews were, in a way, fortunate. They had been the first to experience Hitler. They had been able to take stock and many had had the chance to emigrate. By the time Austria was annexed, emigration had become more difficult. A great many Austrian Jews had taken the easy way out and had 'emigrated' to Prague. By the time the Sudeten district, the German part of Czechoslovakia, was taken, there was an enormous number of Jews in Prague, seeking desperately for an exit.

Most countries by that time had begun to close

their doors on Jewish immigrants. And my father made the following entry into the *Baby-Diary* which he had kept up in a desultory fashion since my birth:

[Diary Extract]

'...Emigration – suffering for the Jews. Two concepts that determine your fate and ours. We *had* to flee from Karlsbad, although we did so voluntarily and despite the manifold assurances of the good townspeople there that we had nothing to fear. Nevertheless, it was good that we fled in time... Now we live here in Prague, since end of September 1938.

'There's a continuous hurry and chase from one official department to the next, every week new decrees with their requisite documents etc., a chaos in which nobody knows what is happening and which, when all seems sorted out, turns out to have been a wild goose-chase. In addition, there is all the running around to be done to the consulates.'

The Emigration Game

My mother marches through Prague in shoes that have semi-high thick heels. She is small and overweight and they give her a little added height but they cannot be doing her varicose veins any good.

She marches in a brisk yet unhurried way, straight-backed, hands ungloved and balled against the cold, like the brave, plump little soldier she is.

We buy chocolate creams. Mother says that if we pick one with a brown filling, we'll go to England; if pink, then to Scotland; if white we'll have to stay here. I pick a brown (England!), she has the white one. 'Ah well,' she says with subdued cheerfulness, 'Let's try again.' And they do, they do try – again and again and again.

Another Omen

Hanukkah – the festival commemorating the Maccabees. 'The Festival of Lights' my cousins Hansi and Susi call it. We three children stand before the lit candles. Hansi is nine, Susi and I eleven. Hans and Susi sing the appropriate Hebrew song, the *Maoz Tzur*. I merely go tra-la-la and feel a fool. The lights are switched off, only the candles are lit and are reflected in the mirror put behind them to enhance their glow. The grown-ups stand back, in the darkness. And suddenly the mirror behind the candles cracks with the heat, and somebody says in a scared and hasty way: 'Seven years bad luck!' And, true enough, seven years later I was to be the only survivor.

Children with Candles

The children are the candles white,
Their voices are the flickering light.

The children are the candles pale,
Their sweet song wavers in the gale.

Storm, abate! Wind, turn about!
Or you will blow their voices out.

Accounts

'How long can we live on our savings, if you don't work?'

'Half-a-year.'

My father's promptitude surprises me. So he has given the matter some thought. It was to be half-a-year from the time that we left Karlsbad to the time that I came to England and the Germans marched into the rest of Czechoslovakia.

My father runs into an acquaintance who tells us about a sort of soup-kitchen set up for refugees. He invites us to go there. It is in a large room with rows of long tables. We are given a good meal and I am delighted to think that my poor father has saved himself a meal out, when our acquaintance returns and asks him for a contribution. I notice my father gives rather more than the meal would have cost us elsewhere.

My father again. A man approaches him on the street and asks him to buy a fountain-pen. My father declines, but very gently, and we walk on. The man keeps running after us offering the fountain-pen. My father buys it and I see the man making for the nearest cigarette kiosk.

'Look, Daddy, he's buying himself cigarettes. He wasn't even hungry.'

'That's what I would do,' says my father. 'If I had to choose between a cigarette and food, I'd choose a cigarette.' And he and the man who's queuing at the kiosk exchange smiles.

The Return

We receive an anonymous letter from Karlsbad, advising us to come back for our possessions as there is a danger of their being confiscated. We wonder whether it is from Frau Schmidt downstairs. Anyhow, my father takes a chance and returns to the now-occupied Karlsbad. He comes back with a suitcase of our belongings and with my very ancient teddy bear (button-eyed, bald, earless) clutched under his arm. Susi was teddy's name although she had begun life as an Eric. She, the teddy bear, was to remain in Prague, a keepsake for my mother.

The Patriot

Others who returned to Karlsbad or who had stayed behind, are less fortunate. My Uncle Max (uncle by marriage to my mother's cousin) is a great German patriot. He and his son Otto have a tremendous shouting match one day, on a staircase.

'You're a German,' roars Uncle Max.

'I'm a Jew.' Otto shouts back.

It is Uncle Max's contention that, if you play fair by the Germans, they will play fair by you. Returning for some reason to Karlsbad, he is asked for a list of the family's jewellery, which he proceeds to make out in meticulous Teutonic fashion. The jewellery is promptly confiscated and he and his wife are thrown into prison. On his release they return to Prague and when I go to bid them farewell before my departure, Uncle Max is lying in bed, ashen-faced and seemingly a broken man.

The above story has a happy conclusion. Uncle Max and his family emigrated to Philadelphia, where

Uncle Max recovered his German patriotism sufficiently to be denounced as a Nazi sympathiser by one of his neighbours, thereby causing his two sons, who in the meantime had enlisted in the American forces, a great deal of bother.

Lifts

...Ringing top doorbells: asking kindly passers-by the way to the town centre, the Wenzelsplatz: giggling when they are half-way through their helpful, convoluted instructions...

Question: how long does it take for previously well-behaved (or, at least, well-supervised) children to become bothersome once supervision is lifted? Answer: not long at all.

My cousin Susi confides that she has pinched from the Blue-and-White collection boxes (meant to build up the Jewish homeland in Palestine) to buy sweeties. A dashing girl called Judith (she has black ringlets – oh, what heaven!) is planning to put a piece of thread across the street, so that some passing elderly lady can trip up on it... My streetwise friend Trudi from Karlsbad takes me to a hotel where they have the most unusual three-sided lifts that never stop, and which you have to get on to and get off from very quickly. Very daring, we are stepping on and off that contraption. Yet nothing would induce me to go straight to the top. Right at the top there is probably machinery, vast wheels that will crunch the bones of children who venture up. Or else the lifts will turn upside down for their downward journey, throwing any trespassers on to their heads.

Betrayal 1

Word reaches us that a Jewish family from Karlsbad have converted to Roman Catholicism in order to emigrate to Latin America. I, with all the fervour of an eleven-year-old, am indignant. 'How can they do such a thing?' But my parents are sad and thoughtful and say nothing at all. And I realize they are wondering whether, given the chance – the wonderful chance of emigration, they might not be tempted to do the same.

Forethought

A discussion: ought one to be thin and abstemious like Aunt Emmi, thus preparing oneself for the possibly lean times ahead, or should one fatten oneself up, so as to have something to live on.

Expecting a war, Aunt Mizzi has laid in stores and

invites us to inspect her larder. She throws open the larder door and throws back her head with a proud, pleased smile at her own forethought. The adults murmur polite approval. I am disappointed, having expected a veritable Land of Cockaigne, a place of swags of sausages, noble salamis, groaning shelves. The larder is, in fact, remarkably bare except for a modest assembly of soup cubes which, Aunt Mizzi explains, will last six weeks of a siege. Soup cubes are a relative novelty and Aunt Mizzi clearly imagines that each will yield as much nourishment as a soup made of chicken or beef or fresh vegetables. Nobody says very much but perhaps like me they are wondering what will happen if the Czechs do not defeat the Germans in six weeks; and whether Aunt Mizzi will be prepared to share those soup cubes with us.

Jokes

Aunt Mizzi's son, the tall, gangly, ginger cousin Heinz, who is old enough to ask girls to dance with him, has retained a school-boy humour:

'There's a corpse that comes floating down the canal.
It's from long long ago, that is why it's stinking so...'

The song has me (who hates anything ghoulish) in jitters, and him in stitches. But then, death is more than half a century away from him, is it not, and therefore comical, and merely a rumour. His sister, Anneliese, she of the brown bouncing curls, the bright imagination (but she also who has betrayed my dog), tells me a joke that is making the rounds of Prague:

Hitler: Chamberlain, give me Czechoslovakia.
Chamberlain: Oh, all right then.
Hitler: Chamberlain, give me your umbrella.
Chamberlain: My umbrella?! But that belongs to me!

Festivals

After Hanukkah, Christmas. For it is Christmas and Easter, those delightful Pagan/Christian festivals, that we had kept at home, in our assimilated way. This year, the Christmas tree will be a lot smaller but – for the first time ever – my sister will permit me to help decorate it.

I know what I hanker for. I linger at the glittering shop windows of Prague, wondering whether my parents would now be able to afford even the smallest of the Shirley Temple dolls on display. In the end, I settle for the *Little Lord Fauntleroy* instead and make do with Shirley Temple paper dolls.

Phantasies

When I grow up I intend to have either triplets or quadruplets, every one of them looking like my heroine, Shirley Temple. Much mental effort is devoted to their respective haircolour, their names, their personalities.

My own boisterous, stocky self will have been transformed by that time into an ethereally slender, soulful creature whose dark Victorian ringlets will frame her pale, delicate features. I shall live with my husband (a shadowy figure) and the multiple Shirley Temples in a castle-like villa, small roses climbing up its walls, surrounded by park and forest. And I shall be a writer. (Throughout my childhood I alternate between being a film star and a writer.)

A Dissatisfied Customer

She must be an old acquaintance from Karlsbad. We are in a cavernous place, a store of sorts. Although indoors, she's wearing a limp outdoor coat that has seen better days, wearing it against the cold perhaps. And then, after a little conversation with my father about this and that, she suddenly turns on him, pointing to her coat:

'Just look at the rubbish you've sold me!'

But my father has left the little shop and its contents of ladies' coats and dresses behind in Karlsbad. He does not defend himself but walks away, clearly crestfallen.

'Daddy, about the coat, – was she right?'

'No, it was a cheap, dressy coat, intended for Sunday best. It was never meant for everyday use.' And with that reply I have to half-content myself.

The German Gymnasts

In Karlsbad I had belonged to the German Gymnastic Association, the *Deutsche Turnverein*, whose logo, the four F's, was so arranged as to be uncomfortably reminiscent of the swastika. It stood – roughly translated – for 'alert, devout, cheerful and free'. We had sung Father Jahn's hymn: *And this we vow with heart and hand to steel our strength for the Fatherland*. I had hoped devoutly that it was Czechoslovakia we were steeling our strength for.

The Promised Land

Goodbye to excursions into the countryside and dancing around Maypoles. There is Zionism on offer but, at least here in Prague, it is altogether too unglamorous; a lady strumming a dispirited guitar in a basement. Or, in another basement, my cousin Karl, fifteen, in excited mood, making a very stern speech indeed about a return to Palestine, to a gaggle of children. 'And here' he concludes with a flourish, pointing at a blown-up photograph behind him, 'is the man who will lead us there.'

Alas, Karl lacks charisma. But later, an Earthling again and quite genial with it, Karl organises a game in which an apple held under the chin is passed chin-wise from one child to the next.

My mother, an assimilationist, will not even consider Palestine as an option. Although our plight is desperate, although several of our friends will go, she will not consider it. 'I have, after all, *two* daughters,' she says pointedly, thinking of my sister.

Trude

Now although my mother will not consider Palestine, Trude Kohn will, though perhaps too late, for she does not make it.

Trude is an altogether jolly, nonsensical lady, who had once, in happier times, been employed by my mother to take me for walks in the afternoons, oversee my homework and (I suspect) keep me from low company.

Trude must have stayed behind in Karlsbad, after

the take-over. The Jews had been rounded up and Trude had remonstrated with a Nazi who had manhandled her parents. She had been bludgeoned over the head for her pains. When she arrives in Prague she is pale – as ashen faced as Uncle Max after his release from prison. She tries to rally when she meets me again, but she is not her old self. As Hitler prophesied: 'They won't be laughing any more.'

Drowning

Once I am in England, Trude will write to me asking whether I know anyone who might employ her.

'Of course, I am aware that you will first have to consider your mother and your sister.'

And my mother too will write to me in the hope of a job: 'Under no circumstance do I want you to bother your benefactors who have already done so much for you; but if you should meet someone who strikes you as particularly good...'

I am on a raft and they are in a choppy sea. I am eleven, possibly just turned twelve, and they cry out to me – though in the politest possible way – 'If you should happen to have a life-line or lifebelt on the raft, if it is not too inconvenient...'

It is a forlorn hope. Their heads bob on the surface and the waves grow higher and higher.

I'm the one in the lifeboat
After the ship went down:
O never pity me for
The salty voyage home.

I'm the one undrowned,
Though I have come
Sorrowing seas across –
And the rest gone.

'longe sceolde/hreran mid hondum/ hrimcealde sae'
(*For a long time he must move with his hands the ice-cold sea.*)
(Anglo-Saxon – 'The Wanderer')

Otto

After Hitler had annexed the Sudeten, those Jews who had stayed behind had been rounded up. Some at least seem to have spent time in the local prison. My Uncle Otto (one of my father's brothers) had, however, been sent to Dachau, one of the early concentration camps. He was eventually released, on oath that he would not reveal what he had seen there and indeed, arriving in Prague, he keeps dumb. The adults whisper about the matter in anxious tones. I consider it rather honourable of him in the circumstance to keep silent, but forget that he has a non-Jewish wife back in Karlsbad and their two children, who are, effectively, hostages. All he will say is that now he has seen the worst. Lucky to have seen 'the worst' and to have escaped! But then, once he has actually seen the worst, he will no longer be in a position to tell anybody about it.

In Prague, he is able to enjoy a sort of Indian summer. He has left behind the hated grocer's shop (which he inherited from my father's father), and learns to become a baker, finding an unforeseen creative pleasure in the work.

More about Anne

My sister sits on the bed, wringing her hands:
'We'll all perish; we'll all perish.'
My mother expresses surprise. Anne has the least to worry about.

She's young and, after all, only half-Jewish. Anne is the daughter of mother's first marriage to profligate Hans. She is eighteen and very pretty with it.

In mother's eyes, Anne's reserve is ladylike, her silences soulful and sensitive. In mine, she is a stiff little ice-maiden who wants little to do with my father and me. My father, who likes to be liked, is aware of her frostiness towards him and saddened by it, though it is never referred to.

Hurts

Anne had been more dimply and forthcoming with the young Sudeten German lads who had crowded into her room in our flat in Karlsbad, to carry her off on some excursion or other.

But then, in the near future, after the invasion of Prague in March 1939, they will be walking around Prague in Nazi uniform, and the one she loves, the one who had kissed her ('I didn't tell mother about it when she asked – it was much too sacred') will refuse to shake her hand even; and will inflict a hurt that will outlast by decades the capitulation of the Thousand-Year-Reich.

Betrayal 2

My cousin Susi shows me a torch. Here in Prague her friend Lisa and she live in opposite blocks of flats, and signal across the darkness, before going to bed. How conspiratorial! What fun! How cross I am not to be included. For the truth is I do not want Susi to like any other girl much beside me. My cousin Susi is a dainty little person with brown pigtails and a sweet face.

In Karlsbad, it had been her devotion to a girl called Christine that had made me cross. 'Susi idolises Christine,' I confided to my diary, 'and Christine no more than likes Susi'.

And now, eight years on – it is 1946 – I am nineteen and I bump into Lisa in a London street. She has survived Auschwitz, where she did some sort of market gardening which she had quite enjoyed. She's critical of Susi.

Susi had been too giggly for her age, had associated with girls younger than herself. (Did people giggle in Auschwitz? Socialise? Enjoy their work? Or was she referring to their Prague days?)

Lisa tells me that my cousins Susi and Hansi and their widowed mother had all gone into the gas chamber together. Grotesquely, she adds 'Really the best for Susi, you know. She was forever having colds and 'flus.' Observing my reaction, she hastily says 'Well, if you've seen your own parents murdered before your eyes, nothing much registers any more.' But now she's more circumspect. 'I don't know what happened to the rest of your family.' (She knows, of course, and I know.)

Then, as one who is the bringer of welcome news she mentions Terezin where they were first sent, before being deported to Auschwitz. 'Your mother had a good job there, cutting up butter.'
(Surely not for the prisoners? Presumably for the

'Susi'

meiner lieben
guten Grünwürdin
Susli.

Prag, April 39.

guards.) Still, a good job. I am to be congratulated.

Lisa and I have a cup of tea and a sandwich. She is shortly to go on to South America where she has relatives...

Later, an old woman, I go to a class reunion of my old primary school in Karlsbad. There is a general reconciliation and, indeed, most of the children — despite the fact that almost the entire town had been Nazi — had themselves been little angels. They too have been exiled and it is in Bavaria we meet. And here is Christine herself, sixty now, but still with something of her pretty, doll-like face.

I cannot resist mentioning Susi, whose little ghost hovers over the proceedings.

'Ah yes', (reluctantly) 'what became of her?'
I don't mention gas chambers, I may not even have mentioned Auschwitz.

'She didn't survive. She was enormously fond of you: I was quite jealous at the time, you know.' And Christine, coldly 'Well, I used to play with her occasionally.'

And so, in the end, Susi belongs to me. At the back of her photograph, of the small serious face framed in brown plaits, she has inscribed 'To my dear, good friend Gerti.' I am glad it is not 'cousin' but 'friend'.

Dumpling

From the age of six, when we had both started primary school, she had been a Superior Person who had had a regrettable effect on my tear ducts. She had long shed the baby roundness that had given her the nickname, being slim and rather tall for her eleven years.

At home, she had 'knickers to match', giant dolls, an enviable doll's house, a sand-pit in the garden. Her father had a car, and a chauffeur to go with it. He was also, Dumpling had declared casually, after I'd been decapitating dandelions in some meadow, owner of the said dandelions and might very well sue my father for their loss. Dumpling's dog was the superior dog. Dumpling cheated at hopscotch.

When I call on her in Prague though, all I get is a glimpse of their hallway, jammed with every sort of possession and giving the impression of people on the hoof. Dumpling meets me outside. But even here in Prague she has managed to acquire a glamorous possession: a pink transparent rain cape that looks as delicious as a boiled sweet when held up to the light and instead of your commonplace sleeves, has genuine slits on the side that you can put your arms through. But this is the last time I'm to admire her for some time to come.

Dumpling writes to me in England and draws a heart with our respective names on it at the back of the envelope. 'You will always be my best friend...'

Dumpling and I in Karlsbad, tapdancing and singing down the street. Dumpling will send away for Shirley Temple badges. Tapdancing and singing down the street. Sixty years past, sixty years on. Where's my Shirley Temple Button, Dumpling?

The Ballerina

I am astonished to see her here in Prague, on a tram. Is she Jewish, then? (Like Dumpling, only half-Jewish, as I hear years later, and so, like Dumpling herself, mercifully a survivor.)

Helli had been Karlsbad's answer to Shirley Temple. Why, she was practically a professional. She danced on points. She danced to real music. ('Please, Mr Conductor, may we have the music?' prettily, at the beginning of her performance.) She danced to audiences. She had received first prize in a talent competition, when I, with a recital of Goethe, had only come second or third.

Even when she was not on stage, her parents had dressed her in a most conspicuous manner. Little Bo-peep. She teeters along the meadow dressed in blue satin, her blond curls in ringlets under a Victorian poke-bonnet, in her hand a little frilled parasol. Dumpling and I are derisive of such ill-judged finery, but secretly envious and admiring. She walks on, conscious of being a Star, dreadfully alone.

In Karlsbad, Dumpling and Helli live in blocks of flats that face each other. One day, Helli brings out one of her dolls on to her balcony. I suspect it's merely a declaration of wanting to play. But Dumpling sees it as a challenge and brings out a big doll on to her own balcony. And Helli brings out a second doll. And so does Dumpling. Then Helli brings out a third, and so in response do we, Dumpling that is, and I – her humble assistant.

The two balconies are full of dolls. The contestants are like two stags, their horns interlocked.

And now here in Prague on the tram, Helli smiles at me in recognition. A sweet and forgiving smile.

The Stocky Grey Man

We run into another acquaintance on the street: a stocky, grey man whose glamorous, tall (she topped him by three heads), German, trophy wife has scarpered with Another since they came to Prague. She of the Marlene Dietrich voice, who had been cool and kind in her detached, indolent, amused way. He has lost everything at one blow. He does not want to live.

My parents are curiously inadequate to the occasion. He has shed his reserve in his agony; they not. Do they harbour some old resentment? For my parents had moved in humbler circles than his. No one more fiercely snobbish than my mother, she, daughter of the town's leading solicitor, who had twice married beneath her — first the handsome but feckless Hans of indeterminate calling, then my father, son of a corner grocery, and himself, when my mother married him, a shop assistant.

Had my parents felt themselves snubbed in the old days?

They say nothing very much. As he walks away, I want to run after him, stay with him, solace him somehow. 'Daddy...?'

'People who threaten suicide never do it.' But my father is mistaken.

Schools

How proud I had been, back in my home-town, when I'd become a grammar-school girl. One week later though, we had fled to Prague. And here I am demoted to an ordinary school. However, my Czech is virtually non-existent and, after another week, there comes my eviction.

'Why didn't you put her into a Czech school in Karlsbad?' asks the headmistress sternly; for it is a sore point with the Czechs that their Jewish citizens, whom they had treated so fairly under the benign regimes of the Presidents Masaryk and Benes, had chosen to prefer the German language.

Why didn't my father reply, 'Because we were ourselves German speakers, living in a German-speaking town; because putting our daughter into a German school was the most natural thing to do.'

But no, he flounders. And he, the most happy-go-lucky, the least go-getting man; whom Fate and my mother had placed behind a shop counter; he, grasping for an answer, babbles the first reply that comes to his head; intones the mantra which he hopes will do and will mark him out as a 'responsible' man.

'It was good for business.'

And a shadow of disdain passes over the face of the headmistress.

Fragment

My father lifted
a mouthorgan up
to the wind on a hill

and the wind of Bohemia
sighed a few
frail and blue notes

man and child
in a harebell light
frail ghosts ... faint tune

Her Sister the Nurse

There is hardly enough seating capacity in the Jewish-Czech Primary School (back to *primary* — ye gods!) which is overflowing with its additional intake from Austria and the Sudeten district. Now there is no language difficulty, at least not from a social point of view. I learn neither Czech nor anything else and at the age of eleven that does not grieve me. The headmaster is rumoured to be an ex-opera singer.

Considering that she is only my age, she has a remarkably precocious head set upon her short body.

She is a classmate and in our spare time we hang out together. She has a sister who is a nurse and a fount of remarkable information. For instance, did I know that women, once a month... But I too have an older sister. I've known about it for ever. Ah — but do I know how babies are made? In hospital! The way my friend tells it, I envisage it thus:

There are two trestle tables, their short sides abutting. Then mummy and daddy each lie on one of the tables on their backs, their heads pointing in different directions, the soles of their feet touching. Then a rubber hose is affixed to his you-know-what and to her you-know-what. And that's how babies are made and her sister-the-nurse had allowed her to watch once from the doorway.

My mother seems irritated when I tell her. And a few days later I'm removed from the Jewish-Czech Primary school and sent to language classes to learn English instead. By the time the school authorities catch up with the fact that I'm missing proper schooling, I'm on my way to England.

English Classes

The young man in charge of the class is obviously unused to teaching children. Not a real teacher then. He can safely be ignored. Not that I don't want to learn English. Oh yes, I do.

I pore over the text book (too obviously meant for adults) and read hard words like 'waiter' and 'cherry'. And these words are made horrendously more confusing by strange footnotes, spelling out how to pronounce them. Waiter and cherry indeed!

But the young man, by general demand, is required to sing 'My bonnie lies over the ocean' which, curiously enough, I do memorise.

In general though, these English lessons are pretty dull. I turn around to land a punch on the little boy sitting behind me; not in order to inflict GBH but merely to relieve the tedium.

His mother complains to my mother. Unfair. For this same little boy has proposed marriage to me, hollering across the street:

'Gerti, will you marry me when we grow up?'

'Shan't marry an idiot like you!' – Well, fancy making so public a proposal. I hope all the passing grown-ups take cognisance of my sharp and witty reply.

I take him to the hotel with the cunning, continuously moving, three-sided lift which street-wise Trudi had introduced me to. But we are perhaps too indiscreet. Do we belong to the hotel? No? And the august porter shoos us out.

The Curse

My father is summoned to the Head of the Language School.

My father stands in the street, shaking me by the shoulders. I have never known him so angry with me. If I haven't caught up with the rest of the children in a fortnight, he vows, he'll take me out of that school.

A few days later, I fantasise, as is my wont, about my future.

'When I grow up I'll become…' And my father, bitterly: 'Nothing will ever become of you.'

He the adoring one; he who had once carried me shoulder-high through the flat, singing a hymn of praise to me to the tune of Figaro seeing off Cherubino to the wars; he whose darling I used to be; and who himself is my darling still, now says:

'Nothing will ever become of you.'

…And indeed nothing ever has.

A few days later, my mother to my father as we are about to enter the house… My mother somewhat reproachfully, for she herself is, by nature, a brave little soldier:

'Mrs —— saw you weeping on a tram, the other day.' And I: 'Daddy, daddy, say it's not true.'

'It's not true,' my father replies tonelessly, as if to say – 'And what if it were?'

Anon

I was resting my feet between two pogroms
And cooling them in a stream,
When through the tender leaves above
I saw an angel gleam.

My guardian angel: I knew him at once.
He floated about the tree.
Now carry me off and carry me high.
And he said *presently*.

And presently means by-and-by,
And by-and-by, anon.
He settled his halo and flapped his wings;
He kissed me and was gone

Transports and Gifts

And then – a miracle. I am to go to England by children's transport. All, nearly all, is forgiven in our state of euphoria.

One bids a round of farewells ('You never said

goodbye to your great-aunt Hedwig – she was a bit miffed!').

Chocolates are bestowed, several boxes of them; a mouthorgan and a photograph of himself from my 'ever-cheerful, ever-jolly, stout Uncle Walter'; drawing things from an 'aunt' I've never previously heard of. (My mother will be exhorting me, in several of her letters to England, not to forget to send a nicely written letter of thanks to Aunt Ida who'd given me the drawing things.)

Betrayal 3

My mother tries to sound a warning note. We are walking along the street, my mother and I.

'Not everything in England might be as rosy as you imagine.'

I, airily: 'Yes, I know.' But, on arriving home, in a whiny voice: 'Daddy, Mummy is trying to spoil it for me.'

My mother, indignantly: 'Well, really! I only tried to warn her not to expect too much and she actually agreed.'

My mother leaves it at that. My father says nothing. But I am suddenly, appallingly, confronting the abyss of my own treachery and know myself for an absolute little toad.

A Gift Spurned

My mother's mother does not approve of me. Her disapprobation is usually worse than anything my own parents can deliver. I am sent for ten decagram, roughly a quarter pound, of ham. (We do not keep the dietary laws.) Surely, grandmother won't mind if I have a little taste. So I taste a little and I nibble a little.

'That's a very light ten deca of ham,' says my grandmother. Nothing more. But I know that she knows.

On my departure, she wants to pass on to me a Hebrew prayer. I am horrified. To be obliged to learn anything out of school hours is an imposition. (And yet I'd been perfectly happy to learn a Hebrew prayer from another child met, almost casually, on holiday once: such is one's suspicion of all adult instruction.)

Hastily, I rattle through a German prayer learnt once in scripture class. 'Ah yes,' says my grandmother quietly, 'I see you already have a prayer.' She does not scold, she does not even display disappointment. And yet I am aware that I have left something important undone. I leave her and feel relieved and dreadfully ill at ease.

My grandmother frets that of all her grandchildren

'This is the loveliest one', he says…

it is I who will represent (or rather misrepresent) the family in England.

Keepsakes

I linger at a shop window which has wooden heart-shaped brooches on display. Red hearts with folksy little flowers painted on them and a shutter at the centre which opens to reveal a photograph. How cosily my parents could sit in one of those hearts. But my hints are ignored.

Nevertheless, I am given photographs. My father looks at one, taken many years ago, of my mother, my sister and me; my mother then still in her early thirties, myself as a very young child and my sister as a schoolgirl. 'This is the loveliest one,' he says reluctantly, mournfully, but makes the sacrifice. (Who knows whether the photograph will be kept and revered as it ought to be?)

The Blessing

My father, uncharacteristically, tentatively mentions that he might bestow a blessing on me before I leave. He normally leaves religion to my mother who herself holds a rather pantheistic view of God.

'O Daddy, yes please!'

(Abraham, Isaac and Jacob; Adam and Eve; Moses in the wilderness, all those biblical characters together! – and this after all does not entail any mental effort on my part.)

The solemnity of such an undertaking appeals to me. Shall I kneel before my father? Will my father lay his hand on my head and pronounce a certain formula of words?

But somehow, in all the excitement, the blessing gets overlooked. And my father, in concluding the *Baby-Diary* on the day of my departure, blesses instead Trevor Chadwick who is rescuing me.

'You, Gerti, begin a new life. Good luck!'

But good luck is what you wish a passing stranger. And although I shall not see the diary until after the war; and although my father is to write many affectionate letters after closing the diary; and although (distance lending its proverbial enchantment) he'll be addressing – not the disappointing child who has just left – but a much younger one, once so beloved, conjured up by his memory; yet that impersonal 'good luck' lays its chill hand on my spirit. The diary that began in ardour has ended in disillusion. And the blessing that was to be Esau's has been given to Jacob.

Gerda and her father Arnold Stein
Photograph by Arnold Stein

All the leaves have lost their trees.
Child, what tumbled words are these?
Yet I grieve for my lost tree;
Far away the wind bore me.

...The next day, it was English daffodils instead of the snow and slush of Prague. It was pretty shells on the Swanage sands. It was also the day that Hitler marched into Prague...

Dinosaur Footprints
Unearthed In Swanage

Banana or marmite sandwiches by the sea,
And Charles and William in soppy grey felt hats...
We tried our footprints out on the wet sand,
And Nanny unkindly called me *Flatfootgee*...

Commendable Swanage – remembered in soft pastel shades
Under light-blue or sailcloth skies – you had pearly shells,
And fresh air, and stones to climb over, and nursery decorum.
Later, there was a war and the sea was barbed off.

Once dinosaurs stamped thereabouts, picnicked, packed up;
Left antediluvian messages, a sort of *memento mori*
By way of their footprints. Ours are swept away,
And my first English days are March-coloured sea-borne wraiths.

——— • ———